Pla

*Learn how to plan and achieve
your dreams*

Kate Keenan

Pocket
Manager
Books

Published by Pocket Manager
Regency House
2 Wood Street
Bath BA1 2JQ

www.kate-keenan.com

ISBN 978-1-909179-43-1

Previously published as The Management Guide to Planning by
Oval Books.

Images are reproduced by kind permission of Oval Projects Ltd.

Original series editor – Anne Tauté, Oval Books
Editor – Catriona Tulloch Scott
Project manager – Clare Christian, The Book Guru
Book and cover re-design – Philip Jansseune, Walker Jansseune
Image enhancement – Matt Holland, MiH Design
Author photograph – Marko Dutka, Studio Marko

Cover: Finding a way through the labyrinth is made a good deal
easier by working with a plan.

Contents

Plan		**1**
1	**The need to plan**	**3**
2	**Take stock**	**11**
3	**Define your aims**	**23**
4	**Make your plan**	**31**
5	**Carry out the action**	**41**
6	**Measure your success**	**51**
	Check your progress	**57**
	Reap the benefits	**59**
	Glossary	**61**
	Jargon	**63**
	Further reading	**64**
	About the author	**65**

This book is dedicated to
those who would like to manage better
but are too busy to begin.

Plan

Being successful does not usually happen by accident. It is generally acknowledged that devising and following an overall plan has a large part to play in the process.

Making a plan is the activity which gets you from where you are now to where you want to be. This consists of analysing your current situation, deciding on your objectives, plotting your action and then just getting on with it.

Unfortunately, many people rarely find enough time to think about or plan for the future. They will tell you that what happens on a day-to-day basis takes up so much of their time that they have no time left for planning. But, if you are to achieve what you want thinking about your ultimate aim plays a vital part in planning your future.

This book shows you how to get to grips with making plans and offers practical ways to get you started.

1 The need to plan

Planning involves taking a systematic approach to what you are doing. For many people, this can seem simply too difficult. *'Things are always changing so it's not worth planning'* is a constant refrain.

It is true that change is an ever-present factor. And indeed, change is essential if any progress is to take place. However, if you are put off the idea of making plans in the belief that it is not worth the effort, you will find yourself feeling even less in control than you feel now.

Busy being busy

When you are very busy, it is easy to convince yourself that getting on with the job is your first priority. You may think that having a plan is an optional extra which you might get around to at some time or another.

This excuse for not planning may actually be covering other fundamental reasons for not doing so. For example, you may be:

- Lacking the confidence or knowledge as to how to start the planning process.
- Feeling intimidated by the commitment you feel that planning requires.
- Thinking that planning will use precious time which could be better spent on meeting deadlines.

It could be that you may not have fully appreciated the difference between 'movement' and 'action' and how this relates to planning.

Movement
Movement is what you do when you respond to things as they crop up, often unexpectedly. You then have to work hard to overcome them. These usually come in the form of crises which need to be resolved immediately.

Action
Action is far more purposeful. This happens when you have thought things through and anticipated what needs to be done. Action allows you to move forward with confidence and is closely related to having a coherent plan, coupled with knowing where you are going.

Action over movement
Working through the planning process plays a major part in helping you achieve a better level of efficiency. It allows you to engage in action, rather than movement. The fact is that without a plan you usually end up just busy being busy.

This means that things either happen of their own accord or you miss opportunities. Either way, you are not in control. It is also important not to confuse doing work with producing results. Most people find that 80% of their time only produces 20% of the results. The aim is to reverse these percentages through making and carrying out an effective plan.

The importance of planning

To manage anything properly, you need to carry out four major functions, preferably in the following order:

- **Identify what you want to achieve** This means making a plan and detailing what you need to do.
- **Put your plans into practice** This means organising the people and resources your require.
- **Tell others what to do** This means directing and motivating the people involved.
- **Ensure that the right things have been done to the right standard** This means controlling and monitoring the output and evaluating your results.

If these activities are not carried out in this order, you may end up by-passing the formal planning function because you think you already know what it is you want to achieve and how to do it. You may move straight into the more concrete and visible activities of organising, directing and controlling. Each of these three functions is important, but if you do not have a plan, you are unlikely to carry out any of them adequately because you will not be sure of your overall aims.

Planning acts as your cornerstone. Without a firm grasp of what it is you want to achieve, all other activity could be a waste of effort.

When you make a plan, all the other essential managerial activities fall into place. It is so much easier to decide how to organise, direct and control events once you know in which direction you are going.

Good intentions

It is easy to be put off by the thought of planning and what this involves. Often this is because you are unsure about what you have to do or you fear that it entails complex procedures. For example, you might want to:

- **Write a book** Suppose you always had an ambition to write a book and have it published, how could you go about achieving it?
- **Grow your business** Suppose you run a travel agency which is doing reasonably well, but have always intended to expand, how could you do so?

Both situations simply need a good plan to help them succeed. Yet many people think that planning is such a complex and time-consuming activity that they never begin and, for the lack of a plan, do not achieve their ambitions. It is all very well having the intention to do something, but actually taking a first step towards its achievement can be the real difficulty.

The relationship between intending to do and actually doing is rarely straightforward. Many external factors may be lying in wait, determined to prevent the best of intentions from becoming actions.

In general, your intentions are more likely to become actions when you take a positive and resolute approach to planning. The most important thing, therefore, is to affirm your commitment to making a plan.

Get started

Get rid of all your preconceived ideas about making plans. Make your mind a blank. Now ask yourself these four key questions:

- Where am I now?
- Where do I want to be?
- How will I get there?
- How will I know when I have got there?

This is all that planning is about.

Questions to ask yourself

Think about your attitude to making plans and answer these questions:

- Have I ever said, 'I haven't got time to plan?'

- Do I seem to spend quite a lot of my time managing crises rather than getting things done?

- Have I sometimes missed opportunities due to lack of planning?

- Does the thought of planning tend to put me off?

- Do I have lots of good intentions, but find it difficult to organise these into action?

- Do I suspect that having a good plan would make a big difference to my overall effectiveness?

If you have answered 'Yes' to some or all of these questions, it may be time that you gave some thought to putting a plan together.

You will be doing better if…

- You realise that you have been putting off getting important things done for far too long.

- You know you should have a plan to help you organise, direct and control events better.

- You are resolved to make a reality of your good intentions to make a plan.

- You are no longer intimidated by the thought of making a plan.

- You are prepared to set some time aside to do some proper planning.

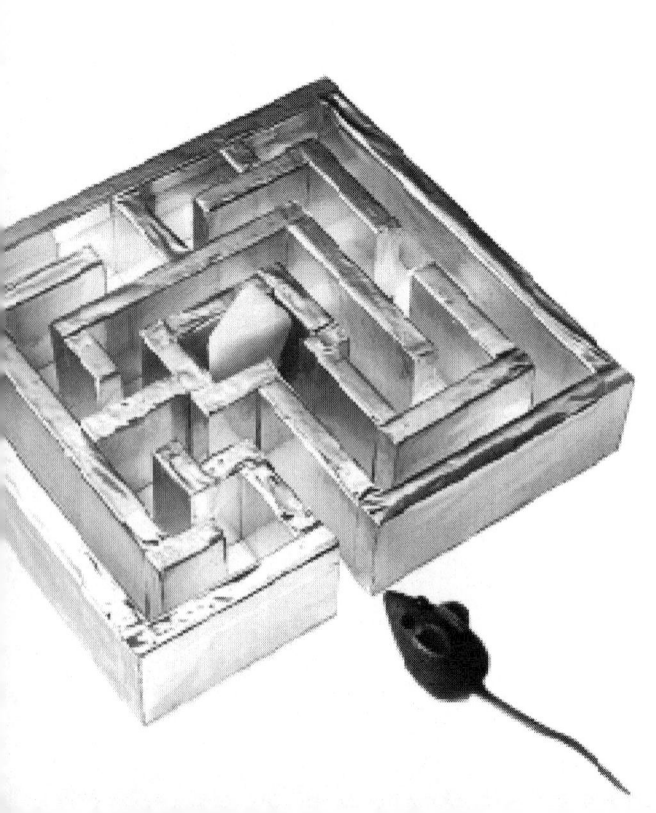

2 Take Stock

The first step in planning is to take stock of your current situation – to answer the question *'Where am I now?'* This is the most important step in the process.

Knowing where you are starting from makes it much easier to determine where you would like to be. If you don't know where you are going, you usually arrive somewhere else. This is especially true if you have not fully analysed your current situation. The best way to find out where you are now is to take a 'snapshot' of it.

The snapshot

The purpose of this first step is to enable you to gain an accurate picture of how things are performing at the moment. An objective analysis of what is happening will provide you with a solid basis from which to project into the future.

There are four key aspects you need to assess and list:

- **Your strong points** Those talents you personally have, along with what is working well in the business.
- **Your weak spots** Those things you can and need to improve; or those you cannot and need to avoid.
- **Your opportunities** Those areas where there are, or could be, chances for you, either in your current sphere or outside it, where you can develop what you want to do.

- **Your threats** Those obstacles which lurk in the background and could get in your way, preventing you from doing what you want to do.

Your analysis of these four aspects will reveal the good and the bad points about both yourself and your current situation. This will provide you with a solid foundation on which to build your plan.

Strong points

By identifying your strong points you gain a level of assurance which will prove vital to keeping up your confidence when other things may not be going quite as well as planned. *'Well, at least I'm good at ...'*

By definition, strengths reflect those aspects where performance is good; for example, your own personal skills and abilities, the talents of those who work with you and the business advantages you may have. Identifying these strong points is not always easy. People are often quite diffident about 'blowing their own trumpet'.

However, if you have not realistically identified your strengths, the plan you formulate may not accurately reflect your potential or that of your business.

Start by writing down everything you can think of about both yourself and also your organisation which could be considered an asset. Make a list under two headings:

- **My/our strong points** Your own and other people's.
- **My/our business's strong points** Those of your business or profession.

Your list might include a whole range of knowledge, skills and facilities which relate to your business, such as:

- The abilities and skills that you (or others) have.
- The quality of your product or service; for example, it is well-designed and customer-friendly.
- Your own and other people's understanding of the business and its possibilities.
- A good physical location or work environment.
- The level of commitment to what you are doing and to that of the business.
- The working atmosphere; for example, it is positive, energetic, productive.

When you complete this short audit, you will find that either your own strengths or those of the business are generally far better than you thought, possibly both. This will enable you to understand your advantages. It may even help you realise you have a great deal to be proud of.

Weak spots

Your weak spots are things that you would really rather not know about, but which, fortunately, are usually easy to identify. They relate to areas where you could and should be doing better.

As before, make a list of those things where performance, both your own and other people's, is not achieving what is required and where perhaps your business is doing less well.

Understanding where things need improvement is important. It may be depressing to dwell on your shortcomings, but honestly identifying your weaknesses is at least as important, if not more, as knowing your strengths. This insight enables you to see what needs attention, for example:

- A level of disorganisation which perhaps gives an impression of not being in control.
- A tendency to take on too much without sufficient resources to ensure successful completion.
- A habit of promising things in an impossible timescale and then finding it difficult to deliver.
- A reluctance to admit that there are some things you cannot do.

Recognising your weak spots is the very first step towards improving your performance.

Acknowledging that there may be limitations also prevents you from trying to achieve things which you should never have attempted in the first place.

Opportunities

Having looked inwards, the next step is to look outwards at what could affect you or your business. You need to work out how external opportunities could help you develop your activities in ways you had not previously considered. For example, think about:

- **Trends in your business** For example, new markets, perhaps abroad – how could they open up opportunities for you?
- **Developments in technology** For example, the latest advances in computers and communications – how could these be of benefit to you?
- **Changes in national policies** For example, health, environment, re-cycling – how might you be able to use these to your advantage?
- **Movements in social patterns** For example, population changes, recreational developments – how could you use such things to do more business?

Think about what you could do in the future to capitalise on any of these opportunities. The answers may not be obvious and may require some lateral thinking. Try exploring your options in a creative way and making connections which are not always evident.

Identifying your opportunities helps you assess how your strengths could be further developed and maybe

used more profitably. Exploring new directions ensures
that you are looking beyond your immediate situation and
are keeping abreast of changes and trends.

Threats
Nobody likes to think about what perils might be lurking
in the wings, but it is important, when taking stock of
your situation, that you face up to a range of possible
threats, such as:

- New and/or existing competition. This could be from
  local, national or online competitors.
- Ever-changing legal or environmental requirements.
- Bad debts or cash flow problems, especially when the
  economy is stagnant or volatile.

If you can confront the things you dread, you will be
less beset by uncertainty – which itself creates a sense of
unease and helplessness. By considering the possible
obstacles, you may well find that:

- Your worst scenario is not quite as bad as you first
  feared.
- You can work out what can be done to solve or prevent
  a difficult situation.
- Your past experience has prepared you for coping to a
  far greater degree than you realised.

By anticipating where things could go wrong, you have a chance to prepare yourself for pretty well any given situation. *'If I can't prevent that, I'll do this.'*

Having a contingency plan is a form of security blanket. It allows you to feel more confident that you will be able to cope should a crisis arise. Dealing with emergencies and crises is not only exhausting but also hugely time-consuming. They need to be avoided at all costs, if humanly possible.

If you give advance thought to what might happen, you not only reduce the shock should it do so, but also prevent a delay in reacting to it. Having a number of remedies ready and waiting is a comfort in itself. For example, *'If my business fails, I'll realise my remaining assets and move sooner than expected to a bolt-hole in France.'*

By facing up to any potential threats, you can decrease your fear of the unknown and have the energy to be galvanised into taking action.

Look at the whole picture

Taking a long, hard look at the overall picture will give you a clearer idea of what's what. For example:

For the potential author

Writing is something many people aspire to, but often do not know where to start. The analysis that the snapshot provides will give a good picture of the current situation.

- **Strong points** I write well, I have a good imagination, and I have a blockbuster of an idea which could easily become a best-seller.
- **Weak spots** I am not very well organised. The idea has been in my head for the last six years and I have still done nothing about it.
- **Opportunities** The novel is about foul play amongst athletes which could be published at a peak period of sporting interest, such as the Olympic or European Games.
- **Threats** My elderly parents now need much more attention from me than previously.

For the travel agency

To grow any business, objective analysis is needed, so the picture might look like:

- **Strong points** We offer a wide range of services. We have a keen, if young, staff and are premises are affordable and well-located.
- **Weak spots** The staff are inexperienced at selling. We struggle with our adminstration systems.
- **Opportunities** The town is growing fast due to a new high-speed train service; excellent sales training schemes are run locally.
- **Threats** We could be overtaken by competition if we do nothing to distinguish ourselves.

These examples indicate how taking a 'snapshot' can give you an overview of where you are now. It can highlight your positive areas, but it can also expose the weak spots which you may need to sort out before doing anything else.

Where I am now

Conducting an analysis of your current situation focuses your attention on the issues which will be vital to your success. However beware of 'paralysis by analysis', which is the downside of conducting any review.

If analysing your current situation indicates that there is a hole in your bucket, then fix it. On the other hand, if you are reasonably content with the status quo, you can start making plans to realise your aims without delay.

Questions to ask yourself

Think about your current situation and answer the following questions.

- Have I identified my strong points and those of others involved?

- Do I know the strong points of the business?

- Am I aware of my own weak spots and those of others?

- Am I aware of the weak spots of the business?

- Have I considered what opportunities are available to me and to the business?

- Have I given any thought to any pitfalls which might be lurking on the horizon?

- Have I worked out how I might be able to cope with the worst possible scenario?

- Have I a clear picture of the current situation?

You will be doing better if…

- You know what you are good at and can identify what your business does well.

- You know what you do not do so well.

- You know the areas that need improving within the business.

- You have worked out where your opportunities lie.

- You can envisage some of the ominous things that might materialise and prevent you from achieving your goals.

- You have worked out a contingency plan which will meet the worst of your fears.

- You have a clear and accurate picture of your what current situation looks like.

3 Define your aims

The second step in planning is about looking into the future and deciding what you want – so that you can answer the question, *'Where do I want to be?'* But it is not something you can just rush out and do, as the answer to this question is not always obvious.

To know where you want to go, the first stage is to be sure you know what business you are in. This is not always as obvious as it seems. What you produce or the service you provide may not always accurately reflect the market in which you are operating.

For instance, if you run a florist's shop, are you in the horticultural business or the gift business? The overall aims of the business will be different. If you are in horticulture, you are likely to be more concerned with the variety of the product. If you are in the gift business, how your product is packaged and the speed of your service will take priority.

Identify your ultimate aim

If you throw yourself into your business without determining specifically what you want to do, you will almost certainly be dissipating your efforts.

Envisaging how you would like your future to develop is an astonishingly effective way to concentrate your attention on what it is you want to achieve.

You do this by defining what your business or profession is all about and where you want it to go. The first phase in this process is to determine your main purpose or ultimate aim, often referred to as a 'vision statement'. No business is too small to have its own sense of purpose.

When you define your ultimate aim, you are looking towards the horizon and determining where you really want to be. You need to identify the underlying, often altruistic, goals of your business or profession, before indicating the more concrete ones. For instance:

- **For the would-be author** The ultimate aim might be: *'To thrill readers worldwide'.*

- **For the travel agency** The ultimate aim might be: *'To give people the time of their lives'.*

To aspire to be simply the best in your field does not comprise an adequate ultimate aim. This is what everyone aspires to, as well as being bland. It leaves too much room for dreaming or for wishful thinking, instead of being a clear statement of intention.

There may also be confusion between your overall purpose and the achievement of your financial goals. For example, *'I/We want to make a million dollars'* does not constitute an ultimate aim, merely a desirable outcome.

Find your way

This second phase of defining what your business is all about and where it you want it to go. This is often called your 'mission statement'. This concerns more the operational, rather than the visionary, and determines the parameters to any form of planning. It should reflect your underpinning business values and ethics. To find out what these are, ask yourself the following questions:

- **What am I in business for?** This is about identifying the rationale of your organisation or profession, its direction and priorities.
- **What do I believe in?** This is about establishing the ethics, principles and codes of conduct governing the activities of the business.
- **What standards am I aiming for?** This is about deciding which are the areas of excellence that are critical to the business.
- **What return am I seeking?** This is about working out the expected outcome from the efforts expended.

The answers to these questions may require a fair amount of thought. But once they are established, they will provide you with a practical starting point for determining the actions which you and your business will take. They will ensure that the plan you make will help you accomplish your ultimate aim.

Involve others

Your ultimate aim also needs to be communicated to everyone involved. Unless there is a clear and shared concept of, and commitment to, what is to be achieved, the chances of everyone pulling in the same direction are minimal. By involving those concerned, you gain a willing and committed group of people who are as enthusiastic as you are about your plans.

To find out how others are thinking about the future, you need to ask them these questions:

- How they view the future of the business: *'Where do you think we ought to be going?'*
- What they consider to be the potential of the business: *'What do you think we could be doing?'*
- What they think should be the overall objectives: *'Whatever the current position, what would you like us to be achieving?'*

The answers to these questions are usually quite revealing. People do not always have the same vision for the future of your business as you do, and what they say can be helpful. On the other hand, they may simply be happy that things continue as they always have.

But if you are not doing very well at something, doing more of the same will almost certainly not improve the situation.

However, identifying whether or not there is a substantial difference in people's perceptions is itself valuable. For instance, if there is no united view of the future, success will be more difficult to achieve.

Holding discussions with all the people involved will explore any lack of agreement in the way the future is viewed. By asking everyone to think about the overall goals of the business, each person will become more aware of the underlying purpose.

Plans tend to work better when those involved in implementing them have been consulted, or at least informed about the role they need to play to ensure a successful outcome.

To make your ultimate aim work, it is essential that everyone in the equation:

- Wants it to happen and also believes it will happen.
- Is committed to making it happen and will not be deterred by setbacks.
- Communicates this belief and commitment to the others involved.

Making sure everyone is fully aware of what they are expected to do, and why, enables them to play a full part in achieving the ultimate aim. Without this commitment, plans will be more difficult to implement; with it, overall success is far more likely.

Where I want to be

Your ultimate aim acts as a lodestar when determining your long-term direction. It establishes the fundamental values which underpin the actions you take to achieve your more specific goals. Working these out and writing them down is a positive act which gets you underway.

Your ultimate aim helps you to keep your eyes firmly fixed on the horizon so that you start off on the right path. It is the guiding light for all your activities.

It is important that you involve any other people concerned early on in this process. This ensures that they are fully informed about the direction of the business and gives them an opportunity to make a contribution.

When the going gets tough, being able to remind yourself and others of where you ultimately want to be gives you a fixed focus and provides a degree of certainty in an otherwise uncertain world.

Questions to ask yourself

Think about how you can go about defining your purpose and answer the following questions:

- Have I decided what business I am in?

- Have I worked out my ultimate aim for the business?

- Do I know what I am in business for?

- Have I identified the principles by which the business will be run?

- Have I specified the desired standards of excellence for the business?

- Have I calculated the returns expected from all the blood, sweat and tears?

- Have I asked others for their ideas?

- Have I written down my ultimate aim?

- Have I made sure that everyone involved believes in the ultimate aim?

You will be doing better if...

- You can answer the question, 'What business am I in?' without hesitation.

- You have identified your ultimate aim.

- You are clear about the rationale which directs your business.

- You can spell out the values which underpin all your activities.

- You know what quality of service or product you need to achieve to ensure success.

- You have worked out the return you expect from your efforts.

- You consulted with everyone concerned when formulating your ultimate aim.

- You have a written statement of your ultimate aim.

- You know that everyone is committed to the same aim.

4 Make your plan

Knowing where you are going in general terms does not tell you how you are going to get there.

If you have an ambition to become a famous author because you know you have an important novel in you, or you want to become the best travel agency in town because you are convinced you can offer the best service, these convictions point you in the right direction.

You now need to tackle the third step in the planning process. This is to make a detailed plan – which answers the question, *'How will I get there?'*

Most plans often look daunting because of their size and complexity. But if you break down your plan into separate stages, the whole thing will appear much easier. Remember the answer to the riddle: how do you eat an elephant? Take small bites.

Identify key activities

In order to make your plan operational, you need to generate a list of the important stages, or key activities, of what needs to be done to achieve it.

- **For the author** The list of key activities might look something like this:

   1. Write a detailed outline, and a sample chapter.

2. Find an agent or a publisher.
3. Make time to complete the book in six months.

- **For the travel agency** If they want to include luxury holidays, the list of key activities might look like this:

  1. Find out about the market.
  2. Pinpoint the luxury destinations.
  3. Train the staff in personalised customer service.
  4. Promote the agency to attract those customers who are looking for luxury holidays.

Having decided on your key activities, the next stage is to commit them to paper. If you do not have a record of the things you need to do, you will almost certainly forget something critical. If you forget to pour the sherry into the trifle, the trifle, for all the effort, will not be the success you hoped for.

The right activities
It is one thing to list the key activities, but it is another to make sure they are the right ones if your plan is to work. Once you have written them all down, check if each activity is the right one by asking *'Why is this important?'* until the answer leads back to your ultimate aim. For instance, the travel agency would ask of the first activity on their list:

Q. 'Why is it important to find out about the market?'
Answer: So we can identify the demand for luxury holidays in our area.

Q. 'Why is this important?' *Answer: So we can offer people the type of holiday they want.*

Q. 'Why is this important?' *Answer: So that they can have the time of their lives.*

And thus you arrive at your ultimate aim. Once you have arrived at the underpinning reason for why you are doing what you are doing, it is much easier to plan the key activities which will get you there.

Plan the action

To make each of your key activities operational, you need to specify the amount of work involved together with estimates of time and cost.

For each key activity you need to make a separate small plan of action.

Work Involved (How to do it)

Asking yourself *'How?'* you can achieve each key activity allows you to break things down into more specific and smaller actions.

This then enables you to generate a range of ideas, along with a list of actions as to how you might go about carrying these out.

- **For the author** Key activity number 2 is to find a publisher. To do this, publishers who might be interested in publishing the work need to be identified. Thus the list might look as follows:
  - Visit library to find books of similar genre and see who publishes them.
  - Check the names with a directory listing agents and publishers and their special subjects of interest.
  - Draw up a list of suitable names and addresses.

  Then a similar list of work needs to be compiled in order to accomplish key activities one and three.

- **For the travel agency** Key activity number 1 is to find out about the market. To do this, it is necessary to identify the types of people living in the locality and their lifestyle.

  This list might look as follows:
  - Check the habits and spending power of people in the area – for example, talking to local newspaper editors and finding out from estate agents what sort of properties are available and selling.
  - Assess which destinations are currently fashionable, or likely to become so.
  - Look back over previous records to see what sorts of holidays have been sold, and to which customers.

  Then a list of all the actions needed for key activities 2 to 4 needs to be drawn up.

Timetable (When it should be done by)

To schedule your key activities, work out roughly when each action can be achieved. When added up this gives you an approximate completion date for the entire plan. For example, 'By Christmas'. From this estimated target, work backwards through the months and weeks assigning specific dates by which each action needs to be completed and build in some 'contingency' time so that any slight delays do not upset the plan.

You usually find when you have finished doing this that in order to complete by Christmas you should have started a month ago or, more likely, last year. You will find that the process of assigning timescales to achieving the various plans of action tends to inject some urgency into their execution.

Once you have fixed these dates you can then assign a definite target date for completion. For example, instead of 'By Christmas', the completion date may end up as 10 January. (Note that it always takes longer than you think.) A workable timetable might look like:

- **For the author**
    - Write to three publishers by 21 May.
    - Identify six possible publishers by 30 April (three most suitable plus three more as a back-up).
    - Complete outline 1 March.
    - Write sample chapters by 30 April.

- **For the travel agency**
  - Hold a promotional evening for luxury cruises on 31 January.
  - Complete catering arrangements by 14 January.
  - Send out invitations on 28 December.
  - Compile an invitation list of potential and existing customers.
  - Make provisional booking of venue on 1 November.

The timetable should be reasonably detailed, but it should also give you some slack to be able to cope with the inevitable contingencies that will crop up.

Costs (How much it will be)

Setting the costs for each key activity is a critical part of planning. You need to think realistically about how much you think you might need to spend in order to make your plan work.

When added up, all these items will produce a overall total which should give you a practical budget. This is the minimum sum you require to implement your plan.

You also need to question the costs so as ensure that items are neither under-estimated, nor outrageously expensive. For instance, *'How much would it be reasonable to spend on postage and stationery?'* In addition, you should work out what gain or return you are expecting from your costs. For example:

- **For the author** There may be some financial costs, but the greatest resource which requires budgeting is likely to be how to balance time between home and writing. For instance: *'Can I expect my spouse to take on the dual household responsibilities for six months to give me two hours of uninterrupted writing time every day, so that the revenue from my book can buy us a luxury cruise in the Caribbean?'*

- **For the travel agency** It is important to know that the costs the plan will incur will be considerably outweighed by the benefits. For instance: *'If we spend £300 on our promotional party, we need to sell a minimum of one cruise in the West Indies to gain the commission to cover the cost. If we can't guarantee at least four more people to book the cruise, then it's really not worthwhile.'*

Write your plan

You will find it much easier to remember all the things you intend to do if you collect your thoughts and then write them down. Until you get your ideas on paper, you really do not have a plan. So list the details of what you intend to do for each key activity, along with the timescales and costs. Get it written, even if it is not quite right the first time around.

Remember a plan is only a working document, so you can expect to go through several drafts before you achieve a satisfactory final version. Indeed if you do not spend time checking and improving, you should question if your initial plan is any good.

Prioritise

When you are satisfied that you have a workable list of key activities, you need to prioritise them to ensure that you do things in the right sequence.

If you do not work out the order in which your actions should be carried out, you may end up working on something that cannot be completed before a more crucial task has been accomplished.

When possible, consult with someone else. You not only get a chance to check your own ideas, but you may also find they have excellent ideas you never thought of.

How I will get there

Spending time on preparing a beautiful plan is all very well but it is a waste of time if you just sit and look at it, or file it, or, worse still, shelve it altogether. Think of it as your guidelines for getting things done.

Committing your intentions to paper is the first step. This makes your overall aims or ambitions seem much less abstract and remote.

But planning is a futile activity without your wholehearted commitment. You have to be determined to do it. If the will is there, the rest will follow.

Questions to ask yourself

Think about putting your plan into action and answer the following questions:

- Have I identified the key activities I need to carry out in order to achieve my ultimate aim?

- Have I worked out the details of what I need to do for each activity?

- Have I set realistic dates for key activities, and allowed time to cope with snags and hitches?

- Have I estimated the costs and is the overall budget reasonable?

- Have I made sure that the action plans for each key activity are in the right order?

- Have I written out my plan?

- Am I using my plan as my guideline for getting things done and not just for a wall decoration?

You will be doing better if...

- You identify your key activities.

- You make detailed plans of action for each of your key activities.

- You set a realistic target date for the entire plan, and build in a generous contingency factor to the timetable.

- You calculate the costs involved and you feel that your budget is sensible.

- You organise your plans of action in order of priority.

- You write down all the details and revise and check them thoroughly.

- You are committed to putting your plan into action.

5 Carry out your plan

In order to carry out your plan, you simply start work on your key activities. But to know how you are doing, you need to keep track of progress.

This means having a system which allows you to check what has been done and what still needs doing. To do this, you need to:

- **Keep tabs on what is happening** You need to do this on a day-to-day basis to make sure that everything is proceeding according to plan.
- **Devise contingency plans** If it is necessary to modify the action, you need to have a Plan B.
- **Act promptly** When you spot that something may not be going according to plan in order to get everything back on course, you need to do something.

Monitoring the action as it takes place is an essential part of your plan. If you do not keep an eye on how you are doing or know how close you are to achieving your various key activities, you will not know if all your efforts are worthwhile.

It is not much use carrying on doing something if there is no chance of it being accomplished. Equally, it is not productive to go on doing something if you have achieved all you can in the circumstances.

Co-ordinate activities

You need a way of mapping your actions and checking your progress. From a practical point of view, the simpler the system, the more successful. Two of the most effective methods are a year planner and a diary, both of which enable you to co-ordinate activities without difficulty.

Your year planner can act as a project management chart because you can log key activities on it which show the various tasks, their duration and completion dates.

By having a simple visual tracking system, it is clear how the plan is supposed to work out and easy to keep an eye on its progress. Mark important dates with a distinctive sticker to remind you that key things need to be done by then. For example:

- **For the author** The planner might show:
  'Finish library research – 20 April' and this date would have a red dot on it.

- **For the travel agency** The planner might show:
  'Complete and check invitation list for mail shot
  – 1 December' with a blue star on the date.

Better still, use your diary to note the dates for completing key activities. By first logging the 'end dates', work backwards and enter various intermediate time schedules by which all the subsidiary tasks require to be completed. This means that if the entry for Monday 20 January states: *'Should have completed outline'* and it is not quite finished, the deadline can either be moved forward by a few days (provided sufficient flexibility was allowed in the plan), or midnight oil has to be burned to complete the work on time. A typical diary page for either entrepreneur might show:

- **For the author**
  10 April
  Library – lunch-time.
  Visit local bookshop – late night opening (10 p.m.)
  Should have a shortlist of publishers by now.
  Weekly Director's Meeting.
  Lisa's birthday Friday – book table/order roses.

- **For the travel agency**
  1 December
  Colour leaflets for cruise promotion should have arrived.
  Confirm venue booking for 31 January.
  Complete invitation list by now.

Because you use your diary every day to view and review commitments of every sort, it is the one reminder system that is pretty well foolproof in ensuring that your plans are progressing – as planned.

Cope with contingencies

Making plans is one thing. Ensuring that they work out as you planned is quite another. Things can happen which are not under your control. In order to combat unforeseen problems, you need to think about how you might:

- Build in a certain amount of flexibility to your time schedules.
- Make provisions to cope with emergencies.

For example: the author may lose a week's work because of a computer problem and failure to make back-up copies. The travel agency may face an unexpected increase in the price of wine, and might want to approach a cruise company to share the costs and meet the shortfall.

In both cases, there is a need to ensure that some form of contingency plan exists. Otherwise, when something drastic occurs, there is always a temptation to give up the plan altogether, rather than adapt it to suit any changes in your circumstance.

Not everything you want to achieve will be achieved smoothly. People who are not directly part of the plan may also have an influence on how the plan progresses.

- **For the author** It is essential to set time aside to write and re-write the magnum opus, while for the spouse, enjoying an active social life may be a main interest. It is important that these different needs are accommodated so that a balance can be achieved between realising the ultimate aim and enjoying domestic harmony. This may mean setting additional time aside in order to go out together.

- **For the travel agency** The preferred venue for the promotion might be fully booked for the foreseeable future. This will not only mean finding an alternative location but also possibly rethinking arrangements .

It is really important to be flexible enough to change and amend your plan as and when circumstances dictate.

Take remedial action

If you find that your progress is not going quite in the direction that you were aiming for, you need to take remedial action very promptly, or your plan could go badly awry.

It is not usually productive to think that if you ignore problems they will go away. More often than not they get worse, so you need to do something positive to solve them.

- **For the author** It seems that there are a great many publishers who publish the sort of literature he or she wants to write. Might it be better to concentrate on finding an agent to channel it in the right direction?

● **For the travel agency** It is found when going through existing customer records, that very few clients in the area went on cruises in the last two years. Is this the best product to promote? Especially if, while doing this research, it becomes apparent that there is a huge market for family holidays in Spain.

For some aspects of your plan, it may be necessary to go back to the drawing board and start again, as what originally seemed a fruitful course of action did not quite work out as you had planned.

Keep control

By identifying the actions required, the schedule to be followed and the expected costs, you have laid down the standards which need to be met and which will indicate successful performance.

For your plan to be effective, controlling its progress needs to play an integral part in the process. If you don't spend some time tracking how you are doing, you could seriously jeopardise all the time you have already spent on making a plan.

It is no good starting a journey with high hopes, only to find that you lose your way and that you have no method of knowing where you are nor how you might get yourself back on course. Ensuring that you know how things are progressing is esse ntial.

Putting in measures to control your plan can require as much energy and attention as you required setting up the plan in the first place, but it keeps you on track and able to assess your success.

How I know I am getting there

Just because you have committed your plan to paper does not necessarily mean it will happen.

Managing and monitoring the plan requires your continuous interest. You need to be clear about what has to be done and to co-ordinate what is happening, especially if others are involved.

If you can cope with contingencies or even anticipate problems before they arise, you will be going a long way to make sure that things stay on track. Taking immediate remedial action is the solution should something not go as planned. Implementing the plan requires constant effort, vigilance and commitment.

While carrying out the plan you may also need to remind yourself from time to time of the final destination, your ultimate aim.

Questions to ask yourself

Think about how you keep your plan on track and answer the following questions:

- Do I have a system for keeping tabs on my plan?

- Am I keeping within the timescales and financial limits I set?

- Have I worked out how I would deal with delays or unforeseen problems?

- Am I confident that I know whether things are going according to plan?

You will be doing better if...

- You check your actions against your plan.

- You use your systems to keep track of progress.

- You stay within your budget.

- You allow enough time in your timetable to get done what needs to be done.

- You think about how you might be able to cope with the inevitable contingencies.

- You can clearly see how the plan is progressing.

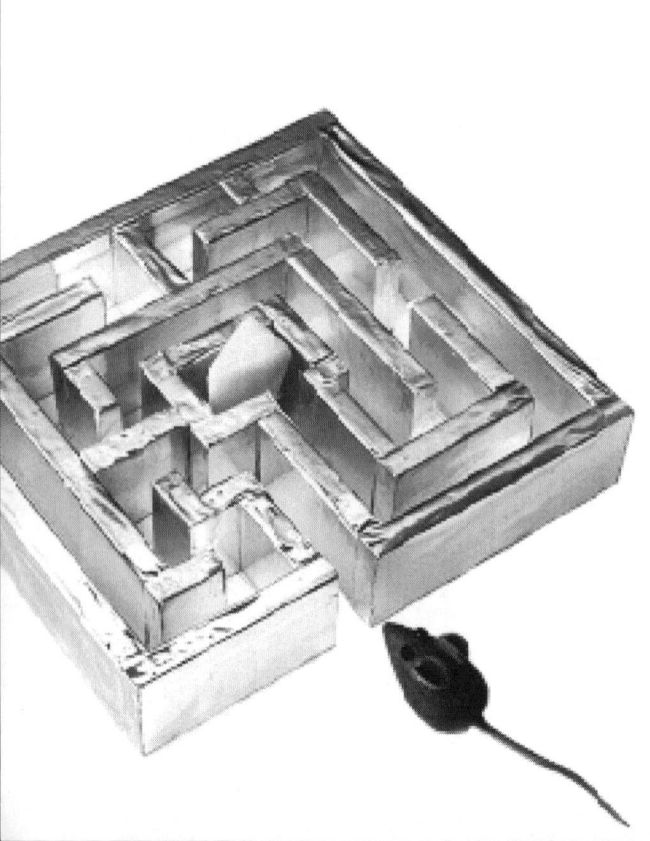

6 Measure your success

The final and most important step of the planning process is to measure the success of your plan. This is done by examining how well you have achieved your objectives – and answering the question *'How do I know that I've got there?'* As well as knowing how well you performed your key activities, you also need to evaluate whether the output from the plan was in line with your ultimate aim.

Judge your performance

To judge your efficiency you have to measure what actually happened against what was planned. In this way, if things do not go as well as expected you know what went wrong and why. The process involves measuring:

- **The quality and the consistency of the work** Whether it is equal to what was planned, or not.
- **The quantity or the amount of work** Whether it is more, or less, than was planned.
- **The timescale in which the work was required to be completed** This is the one thing you are likely to be well aware of if all has not gone according to plan.
- **The real cost against the predicted costs** With good planning, these will not be far apart.

In practice, outputs might look like:

- **For the author** Thorough research, well-presented letter and excellent outline *(quality)* submitted to six chosen publishers resulted in four rejections, one no-reply, and one expression of interest *(quantity)* in the idea but suggesting a complete reworking of the text. The whole procedure took longer than planned *(timescale)* because replies were so slow and endless chivvying was necessary. This incurred extra expense as there were many more telephone calls and letters involved *(real cost)* than estimated.

- **For the travel agency** The cocktail party was much enjoyed with excellent eats and wine *(quality)*; 30 people arrived which was 50% more than accepted the invitation *(quantity)*. This meant that it was more expensive than planned *(real cost)*, but two people made a booking on the evening itself and another four booked the following week *(timescale)*.

Evaluate your effort

Evaluating your plan helps you to decide what to do next. You need to decide whether your plan was effective, and if so, whether you will do it again or perhaps do it differently. Take as objective a view as you can. The effort you put in to achieving your plan and the results you get out are not always equal. You can sometimes find that very little is achieved from a huge amount of effort.

This means you need to take stock and decide what part of the plan needs radical revision. But you also need to bear in mind that the results may have been affected by outside influences – things which could have modified the outcome of all your efforts and which had nothing to do with your plan.

Conversely, for very little effort on your part, the results may be quite spectacular. This may be because you did exactly the right things at the right time as you were in touch with what was needed. Or it could be that external factors were enhancing the results.

- **For the author** The initial results were disappointing. Despite a great deal of carefully planned effort, there was little reward. This was due, in part, to the author's unfamiliarity with the publishing world. During this phase of the plan, experience and knowledge were acquired as to how to approach things more effectively. The author decides not to repeat that part of the plan which relates to finding a suitable publisher, but to try to find an agent instead, and builds a large contingency factor into the estimated costs.

- **For the travel agency** Much more than was expected was achieved as they had targeted the right market. But their efforts were also aided by the fact that the weather had been appalling for the previous month and people were desperate to have something wonderful to look forward to. While they achieved more than their minimum requirement of bookings, they also need to be aware of the part external factors played in their success. The travel agency decide to capitalise on their success and to specialise in cruises which the more affluent newcomers to town are prepared to buy. They now want to increase their reputation for quality service – which of course means making another plan.

Evaluation is an important final part of you plan. It gives an idea of the areas that went well and highlights those where you might want to do things differently next time.

How I know I am there

Once you have measured and evaluated the results of your plan, you are in a position to judge if what you have achieved was worth the effort.

Planning is a continuous activity which needs to go on all the time if you are to achieve anything. By knowing where you are now and keeping your ultimate aim in mind, you can decide where you next want to be and work out a further plan of action.

So get stuck in and start another one.

Questions to Ask Yourself

To judge the success of your plan, you need to answer the following questions:

- Was the quality achieved what I expected and desired?

- Was the quantity sufficient?

- Were the costs within the budget?

- Was the plan completed on time?

- Would more effort have achieved better results?

- Was the plan sensible?

- Was the plan worthwhile?

Your answers to these questions will either help you make adjustments to ensure things work out as planned next time, or they will enable you to feel very pleased with yourself.

You Will Be Doing Better If...

- You measure your actual performance against your planned performance.

- You evaluate the results.

- You understand the importance of planning.

- You feel you are well on the way to becoming a confident and effective planner.

- You are now ready to develop further plans.

- You are considerably closer to achieving your ultimate aim.

Check your progress

If your plan does not quite work out as anticipated, it is unlikely that fault will be found with the whole plan. It is more likely due to one specific area not being quite right. The key aspects of planning you might need to consider more carefully are:

Know your starting point

It may be that you did not seek out, or perhaps were not given, the correct facts as to your current situation. Or possibly that you did not fully assess exactly what was needed. If you did not obtain enough information at the start, evaluate the current situation, or identify your opportunities, you may have built your plan on quicksand. The amount of initial preparation you carry out before you start is the most critical factor in ensuring the overall success of any plan.

Set goals

If you find that at some point you have deviated from your original goal, it may be that you did not set course in the right direction at the outset. If you did not correctly identify your purpose, or failed to keep your goal in sight at every stage of planning, then your key activities may well be misconceived and you could find yourself heading in the wrong direction.

Monitor your plans

If your monitoring process was not correctly set up, you may well have found it difficult to check which parts of the plan are working or whether some parts worked better than others. As the effort you put into achieving your key activities is the essence of making your plan work, it is important to keep close track of your progress. Remember, not all effort necessarily produces the desired results. This is why an effective monitoring system forms the backbone of planning.

Schedule activities

If 'not having enough time' was a cause for concern, make sure you build extra hours, days, or weeks into your timetable. Make sure that the amount of time you allow for each stage of your plan is sufficient for you to complete it and keep track of your activities as you are carrying them out.

Achieve results

If your plan did not produce quite the results you were expecting, you need to know how and where there might be room for improvement. You will find it difficult to judge the full effect of your plan unless you make sure that you measure the outcome of your efforts. This allows you to make adjustments to any further plans. It also goes a long way to guaranteeing future favourable outcomes.

Reap the benefits

Having a good plan plays an integral part in all your work-related activities. It is not an optional extra to be used for special occasions and holidays.

Formulating a plan does not have to take an enormous effort. Nor need the prospect of planning be so daunting that you never get started.

The benefits of making a plan are that:

- You become much clearer about your ultimate aims.
- You are more confident that your day-to-day action is purposeful.
- You are able to analyse your situation objectively.
- You become more methodical in your thinking.
- You are able to capitalise on the strong points of your business or profession.
- You can minimise your weak spots.
- You get things done.

Planning is the compass that helps you determine what needs to be done today to make it more likely that your aims and objectives will be achieved tomorrow.

With a plan you have greater control, can make things happen positively and are far more likely to achieve that elusive prize, success.

Glossary

Here are some definitions in relation to making a plan.

Action
Purposeful movement which requires effort, the only way to achieve aims and objectives.

Commitment
Action long after the enthusiasm has left you.

Control
The exercise of personal influence required to ensure that things are working out the way they were planned.

Cost
Expenditure essential to carrying out the plan.

Intentions
What your mind is paved with. In an ideal world you would translate them all into action.

Key activities
Imperative areas of action. If you don't know what these are, you cannot make a successful plan.

Measurement
Objective assessment of results.

Movement
Purposeless activity which gives the rest of the world the impression that you are busy doing something.

Opportunities
Likely openings which need to be identified.

Organising

Working out what is needed, taking necessary action and being prepared.

Plan

System that brings ideas to fruition by design rather than by chance.

Quality

Standard of excellence which meets all expectations.

Resources

Assets which should be brought to the aid of all plans. Rarely used to best advantage.

Strong points

Advantages which form the foundation from which to develop your plan.

Standards

Yardsticks against which to measure performance.

System

A simple method for tracking your progress on a day-to-day basis, for example, a diary.

Timescale

Pace and duration of a plan. Accurate estimates of this are vital to its success.

Threats

Hidden menaces which need to be recognised.

Weak spots

Defects which can prevent you from getting your plan off the ground.

Jargon

There are a number of popular jargon terms which often crop up in relation to putting a plan together which are useful to know about:

Critical Path Analysis
A fancy way of monitoring your plan's progress.

Mission
A bland statement of business aims, usually compiled by committee with the lack of clarity attendant upon such decisions.

PERT
Programme Evaluation Review Technique; an acronym for keeping track of progress.

SWOT
Strengths, Weaknesses, Opportunities, Threats; an acronym for the snapshot test.

Vision
The brainchild of one person, usually in need of heavenly aid.

Further reading

Plan provides you with an overview of the basic skills you need to develop and enhance in relation to how you make things happen purposefully in the future.

Below are some other resources which you might find useful when seeking to develop and augment your planning skills further.

Michael Anderson and Jane Khedair (2009)
Successful Business Plans: Get Brilliant Results Fast, Richmond, Surrey: Crimson Publishing.

Brian B. Brown (2006)
Writing a Business Plan and Making it Work: The Easy Step by Step Guide, Hayling Island: Rowmark Limited.

Vaughan Evans (2011)
FT Essential Guide to Writing a Business Plan: How to Win Backing to Start Up or Grow Your Business (The FT Guides), Harlow: Prentice Hall.

About the author

Kate Keenan, CPsychol, AFBPsS, BA, BSc, MSc, MPhil, has over 20 years experience as a chartered psychologist and is expert in the areas of occupational and organisational psychology. Kate specialises in promoting psychological wellbeing in the workplace. She has worked extensively with corporate and independent businesses, devising strategic management programmes that enable them to identify and resolve managerial issues – from personnel selection and individual assessment to team building and attitude surveys.

She also works as a mentor and coach, helping entrepreneurs, business owners and other people maximise their prime asset – themselves. Kate offers a series of practical and transformative evidence-based strategies designed to help people make the most of their opportunities, both business and personal.

She has a post-graduate qualification in Mental Health Studies from Kings College, London and currently lives in Bath.

In terms of being able to make a good **plan**, she says:

'I am convinced that being able to plan well plays a central part in successful management and I am well aware that putting good intentions to work takes a degree of discipline, but is also thoroughly rewarding. So much so, that I have even been known to make plans for the fun of it.'

Pocket Manager Books

'Especially for people who neither have the time nor the inclination for ploughing through the normal tomes...'

Personal development
- Assert yourself
- Handle stress
- Make time
- Manage yourself

Essential business skills
- Manage
- Plan
- Recruit
- Run meetings
- Solve problems

Productive relationships
- Communicate
- Delegate
- Motivate
- Negotiate
- Understand people

More information about these books available at...
www.kate-keenan.com